BECAUSE YOU TOLD ME TO WRITE

K ATHERINE C AVA

PAGE PUBLISHING
Conneaut Lake, PA

First originally published by Page Publishing 2023

ISBN 979-8-88960-479-2 (pbk)
ISBN 979-8-88960-485-3 (digital)

Printed in the United States of America

To my mom, who supports me even when she thinks my decision is iffy.

To my friends, who listened to me and told me I was right, even if I wasn't.

To Ms. Thomas and Mr. Spinelli, who inspired me in every way possible and appreciated whatever I had to say and create.

And to you, the person who told me to write, thank you.

preface

High school. What an interesting place—a building full of new people and anticipation of new experiences. Within four years, people can thrive or hit rock bottom. Others, like me, choose to live in the middle of the two, holding on for dear life, screaming at yourself to never let go, but then you meet *them*: the person that makes you believe that everything will be okay, even if it only makes you hurt more.

Inside these pages, you will find implications of suicide, self-harm, and mental disorders. Some might deem these words as "disturbing" or "uncomfortable."

However, these words are just my life.

the introduction

I wish I didn't feel like this. I wish I didn't think this way. I wish I wasn't paranoid. I wish I didn't listen to you and believe everything you told me. I wish I didn't still miss you and the way you messed with my head. I wish I never met you, and I wish you never left. I wish you were still here when I needed you the most. I wish you didn't lie, and I wish you didn't cheat. But most of all, I wish I wasn't so weak.

I wish I didn't feel like this. I wish I didn't think this way. I wish I wasn't here, and I wish you always stayed. I wish you didn't act that way, and I wish you weren't so annoying. I wish we never spoke, and I wish we never met. I wish we didn't end like this, and I wish you all the best. I wish that last sentence was true, and I wish I didn't still feel so blue.

I wish we never met. I wish you never left. I wish you never moved the hair from my eyes, and I wish you didn't kiss me goodnight.

I wish I didn't feel this way, and after all this time, the only thing I wish you didn't do was give me a reason to stay.

I wish I didn't feel like you did all this to give me a reason because you told me to write.

yes

Sometimes people ask me if I miss him.

And I always say yes because he was a part of me for a long time.

Yes, I miss him because we never got a proper goodbye.

Yes, I miss him because he taught me not to care about what other people thought.

Yes, I miss him, but I know he doesn't even know me anymore.

Yes, I miss him, but I know he doesn't feel the same.

Yes, I miss him, and I wish he was here with me.

Yes, I miss him, but I hate him.

Yes, I miss him, but I never want to see him again.

Yes, I miss him, but he will never miss me too.

tough night

It was a tough night,
But I can still sleep through the night.
Rain falls down through the sunlight.
It was a tough night.
I'd like to see your smile,
But I wouldn't be alright.

She was the light from above
When there was no hope left for me.
She was the bandage that covered the blood
    escaping from out of my reach.
She was the smile that goddesses were jealous of.
When she saved my life, she gave half her smile to
    me, and I gave her half my frown left.
She was the pills that kept me alive.
One dose was enough to let me survive throughout the night.
She was all the amazing jokes ever told,
Each one making you laugh in a different way.
She was a song that played throughout my head
Day in and day out,
Letting it be the only touch of reality that I had left.
She is the only one I have left
Because everyone else left me to be with someone who is happier.
I feel guilty that she stuck around for so long
Because I'm sure she's traumatized from what she experienced,
From what she heard,
From what I said.
But here she is,
The lightning in the gloaming.

it's never forever

Nobody said it would last forever,
But you did what you did, remember?
I didn't want to tear you apart,
But you did it first.
I wanted to die by your side
And never be apart from you,
But nothing here lasts forever.
Everyone but you remembers
The mistakes you made last September.
Please don't drag me around forever
Because this isn't going to be forever.
Please let me remember
Why the mistakes you made were so clever.
I just wanted to get there,
But I know this wasn't gonna last forever.
Even if we tried to get there,
I know we weren't gonna be together forever.

fly high

I saw him sink into the ground.
Yes, I was there to watch him fall down.
Did you look up to see your family all falling apart?
I know it's not fun for you.
It's not fun for me too.
I guess I can't accept you're actually gone.
I go to call you, but there's never an answer,
Just endless ringing on the other line.
I know this isn't what you wanted,
But the pain was taking over your body,
A poison spreading throughout every vein.
I wish I could see you again,
But I know that won't be for a while,
So right now, fly high.

alarm

He died when I was in seventh grade.
He told me that was going to happen.
He counted down the hours, days, and minutes,
Set it according to the clock,
And when the alarm started sounding,
You were gone when you were supposed to be.

I guess you're not a liar.
Welcome to heaven.
You deserve it
For not lying and stabbing me in the back.

delusional

I see him.
Everywhere.
I see him in the middle of traffic
When I'm on the freeway.
I see him standing on the sidewalk
When I fly by him in my car.
I see him walking towards me
In the middle of nowhere or in a crowded area.
　　My heart rate rises every time I see him.
　　I see him so much,
　　Which is crazy because he's dead.

confusion

All these things that are going on in my mind
Just seem a little incorrect.
So I'm sorry
If I complain as much as I think I do in my head.

text message no. 1

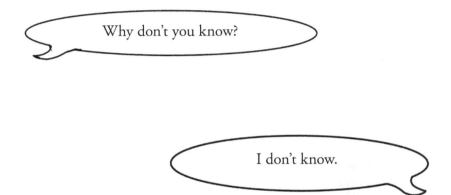

letters

Hey,

I thought you forgot about me.
You've been ignoring me all week.
I know you're not feeling well,
But I'd like to see your face again.
I miss our long conversations,
And you making me laugh.
Sometimes times get rough,
But I always catch myself looking back.

We somehow make it back to each other.
So call me when you see this.

I love you even though I know you don't love me.

Love,
Your "friend"

memory

People say they miss my smile that lit up multiple
    rooms even when I was by myself,
Crying and screaming in the mirror, blaming
    myself for not being good enough.
I don't know what to say when they say they miss my smirk.
So I just say,
"Look at the photographs that we took together.
Remember all the good times we had
Because the smiles aren't coming back until people become kind.
So remember my laugh in your memories because
    forever lasts forever when you're stubborn enough
    to never forgive or forget your entire life.
So remember my smile in your memories because even when the
time is up, the smile will never creep its way back onto my face.
Even after all these years, when I'm alone in my room,
I still go to my mirror, and I tear open the lines that I closed so long
ago, and I forget why I stopped smiling to begin with.
But then I check the comments and articles and everything mean
said about me, and it all comes rushing back.
Every reason, every attempt, every night that
    I spent crying in the dark.
So remember my smile in your memories because even when
    the time is up, the smile will never creep its way back onto
    my face because I remember the rush of emotions it gave
    me, and I feel better when I don't feel anything at all."

listen

Can you hear me when I say
"Please don't leave me?"
I'm not done with you when I say
"Please still love me."
Hold me tight when I say
"I'm scared you'll leave me.
So, don't let me be alone,
Because I want you still.
So, please don't leave me behind
When I still chase your heart."

for granted

I wanted to love you, but you made me hate you.
I wanted to keep you, but you made me leave you.
I guess things won't work out.

Throughout all this time we had together,
Every day was my favorite pleasure.
You wanted to leave, but then you remembered
The tension between us was an adventure.

I wanted to hate you, but you made me love you.
I wanted to leave you, but you made me keep you.
I guess we can get back together.

Throughout all this time we had together,
I wanted to leave, but then I entered
The tension between us as an adventure.

Throughout all this time,
We can just stay here forever.

wall

I'm sorry that I set my boundaries with you.
I'm sorry that you're upset I don't share
my whole life story with you.
I'm sorry about all of it.

But it's hard for me to care
When you never actually cared for me.

dark mistakes

Sometimes, things are just better in the dark.
I don't want to see my future without you there.
I know we went through some dark times,
But I would do anything to get you back
Because I love you,
Because I miss you,
Because I made a terrible mistake.
I know you don't want me,
But it would be great if you did.

You said you wanted me
forever,

But you also said to get off my
phone.

So I don't know what you want
me to do.

I guess I'll just wait for you to
come talk to me.

fools

It hurts me to tell you that I don't love you anymore.

I can feel you looking at me when I decide to look away.

It hurts me that I broke you down.

I could lie awake at night, thinking about what we could've been.

It hurts me to hurt you,

But I have to walk away.

Didn't I have to hurt when you left me first?

I don't feel guilty about the things I said.

I told you that you lied and tried to convince me otherwise.

You were foolish,

But so was I.

I guess we can get back together and be fools forever in time.

indecision

I don't ignore you;
I only adore you.
I hate you,
But I love that you hate me too.
You'll learn to love me,
Like I once had to do.

lost

I want to say I remember you kissing me in the rain,
But we didn't get that far.
In fact, I remember nothing was perfect,
And pain was a constant feeling in my chest.

I remember you being my "home away from home."
I remember you being the person I went to
When I had nowhere else to go.

need

You could've said "You have my heart forever."
Or "I'll never leave you, baby girl."

As the tears fell
And midnight struck free the spell,
You left before I got the chance to say
"I love you. Never leave me.
"I don't care if it's the worst love you've ever seen.
"I just want you forever. I don't need an endeavor.
"Don't leave me alone 'cause you're all I need
When I thought I only needed me."

louder than words

Sometimes I feel like I'm crazy,
That you always hated me.
But when I'm crying alone,
You always blow up my phone,
Telling me to come over,
Telling me, "I always need you."
But your actions speak louder than your words.

falling from grace

The art room—silent, sweet, and peaceful.
The beautiful devil with an angel halo tightening around her neck.
A slithering sense of gossip fills the aroma.
Everyone in her sight suddenly turns to stone.
She strolls in and shatters the glass in the window.
"I have something to tell you. Come over
here so I can whisper it slowly
in your ear.
It's about my friend. It's a strange thing to hear.
She's faking it all. She doesn't really feel that way."
High school children come and drown the truth in fate.
She lurks through the hallways like a snake going for their next
kill.
Wow, what a thrill.
She gossips till her heart is content.
It sucks that she lives in my mind but still doesn't pay rent.
She was real, but now she's nothing more than a convenience.
The secret she said she would never tell or show.
"I would tell you everything, my dear, but then the whole world
would know."
I'm talking to her, and my knuckles are curled and white.
This conversation is going in such a fast pace.
I'd like to tell you the truth, but in the end, I would end up falling
from grace.

creative urge

Art of manipulation,
Messing with me is such a temptation.

23

overshare

I don't want to write about you anymore, but now I live my
life telling our story—expecting to get sympathy from
people who don't care about me either.

middle of starting over

You said you loved me then,
But I don't affect you now.
What's the point in being here
If I have no point at all?

Waiting all my life, apparently wasting my time.
I wanted to end;
I wanted to leave it behind.
But you're here now;
I guess I'll survive.
I'm waiting to start it over.
I'm waiting for this to be over.
You see me falling down;
I can't slow it down.
There's so much pain;
I just want to drown.

I thought you would save me but instead knocked me down.
Waiting all my life, apparently wasting your time.
I wanted to end.
I wanted to die.
I wanted to leave all this behind.
I'm waiting to start it over;
I'm still waiting for it all to be over.

hope's for suckers

I wish that you would say
that you love me the same.

I hope that you'll be my baby,

But I guess we're stuck
waiting for now,

But it'll happen one day.

overthinking

I'm stuck in my room, and I'm
going insane.

I want to see your face so I can
heal from the pain.

I would go outside, but there's
nothing to gain.

So I'll just sit here, stuck in
my own brain.

do you remember?

Do you remember when you said you loved me?
And that you'd never stop until the end of time?
Do you remember when you said you'd never leave me till
The day we both die?
Do you remember
Everything you did to me and every scar you made on me?
When you said you'd never hurt me?
That I was being overdramatic, that I was
      making our love traumatic?
I pulled up my sleeve, and there was cold, hard proof
Of everything you did to me.

When a blade touches skin, no matter which way you cut it,
It all bleeds the same.
You tried to convince you didn't
Find a knife and hide it in my back.
Do you remember
Everything you did to me and every scar you made bleed?
When you said you'd never hurt me?
That I was being ungrateful, that the way I treated you was hateful?
I pulled out receipts and showed you everything you did to me.

No matter how sharp you make the knife,
You can't kill me 'cause I'll survive.
No matter how many times you load the gun,
You can't kill me 'cause I'll survive.
No matter how many times you kick me down,
You can't kill me 'cause I survived you already.
Do you remember?

advice told from everyone, everywhere

Forget about the past, and focus on the future.

In the past, you made mistakes; but in the future,
You fix your mistakes.

hard times

I walk with you and stand by you.
You beat me up and tear me apart.
You break me down and steal my heart.
And you're still here.

I wish you would leave me here to decay,
But you're still eating me away.
What did I do to deserve this?
You said I was your treasure;
I'm not appreciating the transgressor.
Where am I in your heart?
Because I didn't do anything to deserve this pain.
Do you expect me to stay tied up in this chain?
I was told to be careful around people like you,
Yet I stayed
Just for you.

It would be nice to hear your voice in my ear.
I want to get up and try again, but you ran away.
I want to see your face, but you live in outer space.
I want us to be forever,
But you ruined it for us forever.

my sincerest apology

Sorry,

I'm truly sorry that you had to walk so far to
just apologize for what you did.

Maybe next time you'll learn from your
mistakes.

But you won't.

And I know that because you've done it before,

And you'll do it again.

So again, I'm sorry that you can't control
yourself from screwing over everyone you know.

Please forgive me.

effect

Making poems
That read like songs,
Thinking that singing away the pain
Will solve every issue
Or will make me belong.

When I read them out loud to you,
You tell me I'm talented,
But my words were cruel,
Rhyming about the trauma
That you shoved down my throat.

Shouting and tears dripping down my cheek,
Lying on my bed,
Head turned to the side,
Puddles forming in my ear,
But of course,
Everything that happened was my fault.

prequel

I made this poem when I was eight,
Hoping people would relate.

What you're about to see next
Is not my best work,
But it certainly isn't the worst.

Please don't judge me for this sad, sad poem
When I loved someone
Who didn't love me in return.

If you can relate,
I'm sorry for much,
But just remember,
Don't sweat the small stuff.

i remember when i was eight

I remember the day I fell on the ground;
You picked me up and turned me around.
I remember the day you walked me to the office grounds.
We walked up to the open doors of the classroom,
Brightness in the sky.
You said to me, "Nice try."
But I remember life before, struggling, stuck, locked in doors.
I remember the day when you left me behind when I was stuck
Somewhere in the night sky.
I remember that day, and I remember you.

ZR

Even after all your lies and
manipulation, I still said "sorry."

I did nothing wrong, and I still said
"sorry."

I spilled my heart out to you when I
was happy, and you broke my heart
because you couldn't be loyal or end
things like a mature person, and I
still said "sorry."

living

Every time I go to jump off the cliff,

You always save me.

"I just want this to end."

But you need me

More than I need to be

Alive.

backstabber

I'd like to think that your stab in the back
    didn't go straight to my head.
But the moment I heard the surge of drama,
The paparazzi came running at me,
Resplendent flashes of cameras chasing after the story.
"I'd hate to disappoint, but I'm not involved
    with those people anymore."
They all arched their eyeballs and rolled them
    over the length of the lid.
Walking away since I didn't have anything mean to say.
I didn't have anything at all to say.

Charmolypi: the feeling of happiness while also being sad,
Which is what I get whenever I think about you
And how we considered each other best friends.

Blocking me from your accounts so I don't see the drama.
Getting angry towards me since I'm not controlling your Moira.
Shared my opinions of the situation
And then never spoke to you again
Since you left me and chose him.
But this fact isn't anything new
Since I lost countless friends to him too.

This feeling isn't original.
There's no point in becoming cynical
Since there's no point he should have all the attention in the world
When he isn't anything special.

PTSD

'Cause I'll scream at the top of my lungs,
Trying to make a point.
In the end,
I run.
I'll say "I don't care."
But I'll cry
Till I'm ill.
I'd wanna die
Before I admit it.

I only fear you'll reappear
When my life is good
Without you near.

voice recording no. 1

The audacity of people is insane.

It just blows my mind every time.

I don't even know why, though.

People are deranged, and I shouldn't be surprised.

I'd be lying if I said that I wasn't hurting

And dying from things that didn't need to be said.

despair

I'm sick and tired of being
tied up in this chain.

I want to see your face, but
I would just fade away.

I would go outside, but there's
only rain.

So I'll just sit here, stuck in
my own brain.

judas

Hello, Judas.
I haven't heard from you in a while,
Not since you talked bad about me,
Turning my friends against me.

Hello, Judas.
It's funny to see you here
After you stole my knife and shoved it right back at me.

Hello, Judas.
I think it's funny neither one of us is religious,
But we both prayed to be together.
Yet you were also praying with her too.

Hello, Judas.
I don't believe in personal payback.
I trust that karma will do her job
And sign her name to pain she caused,
In beautiful cursive letters.

So, Judas, watch your back
And sleep with one eye open
Because karma doesn't rest
Until the traitors get
What they deserve.

writer's block

I've always wanted to write poetry or song lyrics,
    but the words just don't fit right.

"I wished you loved me the way that I did. I thought you'd
    do anything for me, but who was I kidding?"

Everything I write just sounds like I'm complaining, like
    the heartbreaks that piled up don't even compare to
    the stuff that other people have gone through.

"I wish you were around when you pushed me on the ground."

That sounds like a little kid wrote it, rhyming
    words at the end of every line.

"I miss you every day even though I know you don't feel the same."

Why should I miss you when you have shown me time
    and time again that I mean nothing to you?

"After all I've done, you still turned around to run."

Of course, they ran; everyone does. Did you really
    think that anything was going to change? Did you
    really think that they were the one?

All these things that I'm feeling need to stop because if they don't, I'm
going to end up shot. I wish I could turn my mind off for a second
because if it doesn't, I think I need to end it. I realize that rhymed. It
wasn't a lyric. It wasn't a poem. It was my true, raw emotion.

backpedal

I always talk about fearing to see you,
Searching the world to make sure
You're not there when I am.

But if one day you find me,
I know I'll go running into your hands.

And I'm ashamed to admit it,
But every shred of this pain is worth it
If I get to see you again,
And we can't become an "us" thing again.

rotten

Seeing my breath turn to fog,
I look in your eyes,
And
Suddenly I'm lost.
Everything that went down
That cold Friday night drown
Is permanently forgotten,
And my heart's still beating
After you watched it die,
Rotten.

burn

People always ask "What's wrong?"
But then never wait for the response.
If I just ended it right now,
Would anyone even care?
Or would they just sit there and stare?
I bet if I walked with my head up
Instead of down,
I would make people speak sounds
Instead of them sitting there and watching me drown.
I love when people bring up subjects and
Sit there silently so they can share to everyone.
You don't care about my feelings;
You just love I can tell no one.
No need to roll your eyes at me.
I know you hate me just fine.
There is no need for me to be relevant in your life
Just so you can hate on me out loud.
Immature high schoolers who can't sew their
mouths shut, everyone hates you enough.
You are adding more gas to the wildfire,
But good thing I love watching the world burn.

karma

There is something strange about how many things
    can happen in such a short amount of time,

Something poetic by the fact that it takes nothing of
    your timeline to change your entire life.

One single second, one millisecond, can and will
    forever modify the course of your life.

Making toast while you take a bubble bath.

Time is a treacherous thing to live by.

Tick, tick, tick, your calendar pages are being ripped out.

It drains you of all your power and your will to live.

But something that gives you power is believing.

I believe that karma overrules any religious entity.

She has been on my side my entire life,

Throughout all time, even when people stuck
    and broke their knives in my back.

There she was, stroking my hair while I cried, telling
    me that something will get them eventually

Even if my timeline will not allow me to be there to see it.

ladylike

Sometimes I wish you would go die in a hole,
But that's not very ladylike of me to say.
"Keep your legs crossed and your mouth closed tight.
I wouldn't want your words to come back and bite."

trapped

I'm not climbing inside that little mind
'Cause all I'll hear is you sobbing and screaming
"Please come back to me!"
You're agitating me, and you're playing her too.
The sirens are silent.
The grind of my teeth is deafening.
Attempts to find a way out of this fiery pit of hell.
I'm trapped in this lightning, so I just stay hiding
Before the lions find me lying in their cage
On an island where I'm rhyming.
Finally got out, now I'm sighing.
The sirens are gone.
I'm done buying your lying;
Instead I will be rising above you
With my fluffy white angel wings.
Your timing was wrong,
But try again
And stop your whining.
There's a girl over there tired of fighting;
I'm sure she'll enjoy all that lying.
Maybe we could become friends
After she dies from giving up her life trying.

war

Either shoot your shot or get shot down.
Bullet hole in my head, my chest.
There's so many things going on in my brain,
But I can't feel any of it since you shot me down.
Man down, man down!
Get some help over here!
I can't get up;
You tied me down here.
Man down, man down!
My body's so heavy;
I can't get up,
So I'll just stay down—dead.
Forever dead.
Inside and out.
My heart, my chest,
All fading away.
Can't speak, can't speak,
Forever holding my peace.
You're dead now,
So just write it in a letter.
I'll speak it at your funeral,
And I'll cry to it, too,
Because everything I went through was war from you.

anxious and depressed

I'm anxious and depressed.
I wonder if I'll ever be alright.
I hear his voice ringing in my ear;
I see him standing in my corner, telling me it'll be alright.
I want to hug him one last time.
I am anxious and depressed.
I pretend like I'm okay when I know I'm not;
I feel like I just wanna die.
I touch his gravestone, wishing he will come back forever.
I worry about everything; my mind isn't right. I have to sever.
I cry because I'm not good enough to keep up.
I am anxious and depressed.
I understand that I should just get over this, but I can't.
I say I'm alright when I know that I'm not.
I struggle with caring about myself and about others.
I try to shake these feelings, but I can't.
I hope that I have some hope left.
I am anxious and depressed.
I remember when things were simpler in my head.
I dream that I can just fade away.
I smile in my dreams,
But when I wake up, I fall six feet deep.
I am anxious and depressed.
It's not the best,
But at least I'm aware of that, one would suggest.

IP part 2

Even when I can't see,
   You're my light into the darkness.
You're all my moods at once.
You're my missing heart piece.
I can't explain what you mean to me;
   You're just all of me.

terrors

Nobody knows if you have nightmares
If you don't share them.

Nobody knows if you're scared
If you don't act like it.

frown

You said I'm forced to see you smile,
But I haven't seen one in a while.

text message no. 2

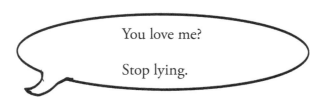

You love me?

Stop lying.

human nature

I hate talking to people.
I'll share every reason why without any shame:

1. No matter how many times they help you or love you, they will always be different towards you when there are others around.

2. It doesn't matter that you would give your soul up for them; they always want more and then say you didn't give anything.

3. They'll expect everything from you, and when you meet their expectations, they won't care.

4. No matter how hard you try, you will never get smiles or applause or an "I'm so proud of you" speech, and you're stuck thinking that you could always be better even if you gave it your life.

5. You could be on the verge of death, and they'd still tell you that you could try harder.

Sharing all these reasons still doesn't help me.
I still feel useless and unloved by everyone I talk to.
I know they will never care for me or give me
    everything the way that I would.
When people are saying that I should be more open and honest,
I think about all these reasons, and I remember why
    I keep my mouth shut half the time.

a million things

A million words did not count.
A million tears just to drown you out.

gossip

I left you because I heard those
conversations you didn't want
me to.

gabriel

I saw a sweet boy in my old class.

It was second grade; his attitude cut deep like glass.

We became friends, so we played and laughed.

As we grew, we talked every day and knew each other's secrets.

I remember all those days you spent teaching me to divide

So my mother wouldn't yell at me because I didn't understand.

Now we're in high school, and things aren't the same.

I never see you because "I'm too much of a pain."

I walked up to you, and you ran away.

Gabriel, I loved you so much. Why couldn't you see that?

Gabriel, you left me for her. I can't believe that.

rules

You told me a million times
Just to get over myself,
To forget all our past fights
Because you didn't really mean what you said,

To wash my hands clean
From all our experiences,
And to set the clocks back in time,
Start from the beginning,
Meet for the first time,
And sit next to each other again,
Have our first conversation,
Maybe change the topic,
And maybe never speak further.

You told me a million times
To stop being overdramatic,
To neglect all my emotions,
And to listen to every word you say,

Every lie as the truth,
Every truth as the law,
And never listen to anyone else
Because whatever they say
Is untrue
Since it didn't come from you.

famous

I remember you saying how much you hated him.
How much you wish you could punch him in the face for how he
treats girls, for how he treated me.
But then, you decided you wanted to experience the heartbreak,
See if it was for you.

You're just like the others.
Everyone knows the details about how he treats girls,
Always saying they hate him for how he talks about them,
But goes off to date him.

There's a thin line between love and hate.
You just showed me how thin that line was when you told me
That you broke up with your boyfriend
And are now seeing him.

When you get heartbroken,
I don't want to hear I was right or see you cry,
Because you know what was coming
Before you got involved with the guy.

addiction

Addiction is a serious thing

That doesn't always mean drugs or alcohol.

Addiction could mean a show that you got so connected to that you don't function anymore 'cause your reality sucks, and a reality that doesn't suck has come to your screen, and you can't stop watching it because everything great is happening until something bad happens, and your addiction just grew because I always cling on to the negative things.

So the lesson here is don't get attached to things when you know there's a dark side to it.

insomniac

People always ask me why I stay up late.
I'm not doing anything special.
My mind is just always busy,
Filled with ideas, lyrics, and rhythms;
Filled with metaphors, similes, and imagery.
My mind never stops because I have an overwhelming imagination,
But that's okay because I have new ideas, lyrics, rhythms,
Metaphors, similes, and imagery
Coming from my mind to paper daily.

questions

I go to a hill just to go away from reality,
To find a place where I belong,
To find a place where I won't be judged by the way I look or the way
I talk or by the stuff I find interesting.

Instead I go to you
Just to get hurt,
To be judged by what I look like, and to be
      criticized for what I find interesting.

So why do I go to you more often instead of going to a hill?

Why do I stay with you when I know you're
      just going away the next day?

Why do I comfort you when I know you won't do the same?

Why do I stay with something so negative when I know
      there is something else so much more positive?

Why do I stay with you when I know you don't truly care about me?
Why do I stay with you when I know there's
      something better for me on the hill?

Why do I stay with you when I know all I'm gonna get is worse?
Why do I stay with you when all my feelings keep getting hurt?
Why do I stay with you when you break me down?
Why do I stay with you when it's not hard to leave?
Why do I stay with you when I didn't need you in the first place?

agonize

Every time I try to be happy,
I always remember that I get less disappointed
When I'm sad.

impalpable

Do you ever look and examine
emails knowing that you're
gonna delete them anyways?

You know what I'm talking
About, and I think there's a poem
in there somewhere.

playground

The world isn't so crazy when you're sick in the mind.
Repetitions and compulsions are just wasting my time.
I go ahead and head to bed an hour before;
I suppose it won't hurt since I'm such a bore.
But when I close my eyes before I'm supposed to,
The devil comes out to play in my mind like a song in queue.

symbolism

The symmetrical snow-white petals growing in my backyard,
There's only one flower there,
The lone wolf,
One might suggest,
But I just said it was underproduction from underground rust.

The bright yellow in the middle,
So perfectly round and detailed,
Almost like it's telling me a story.
Yeah, there is a story.
All this meaning you're trying to find
Is boring me out of my mind.

Sometimes a flower is just a flower.
Sometimes the girl plucking it when she's at her lowest
Doesn't mean that because she feels like dying,
She feels like killing the flower too.
Why would I think of such a thing?
What if I thought that she wanted something
        beautiful to hold on to
Because she felt like the world wasn't capable of providing that?
Again, who would think of such a thing?

Then in my mind came an English teacher,
The one who tries to find meaning about the hole in the tree
And the pebble someone stepped on,
And if I don't find that same symbolism in that same passage,
I'm wrong.
It's always so dramatic,
Which is why I vow to hate symbolism
Even when I use it to write about something traumatic.

tarot cards

Right side up or upside down,
I can make up some nonsensical explanation
From a card that I see every day.

If I sound convincing enough, then you'll find meaning
When I'm just talking with no substance.

"Yes, I got your energy. This is what your past, present,
    and future look like. Does this look familiar?"

"Oh yes, of course, it does!"

I'm reading out of a book.
This card doesn't mean anything unless you
    want to find an actual meaning.

Tarot cards are fake,
But so are you,
And so am I.

So why would I say real problems to a fake person?

Maybe I'm just that petty,

Or maybe it's just because helping you isn't in my cards.

love letter

Dear someone in heaven,

Only if you knew
What was going on in my mind
A thousand times.
Please stop asking me
If I'm mad or fine
When it's perfectly clear
I'm dying inside.

My heart breaks at the thought of you.
I thought you were different,
But you lied when you knew.

Love,
The person you left

regret

I never waved hi.
I never said goodbye.
I never even ever wanted you in my life.

forever

I hope you know that I'll wait forever.
Right here waiting for our life together.

No, you know that I can't wait forever.
Yet here I am waiting for us to be together.

stage fright

Driving past houses,
Every motion sensor light turns on.
All eyes are on me,
No longer lost in the crowd.

Freeze from the attention.
Stage lights turn on.
The crowd turns heads.
Tickets out of stock.

I wish to be lost in the seas full of people,
But I only stand alone.
Beings stand around me,
Eyes glued on my body,
Shaking in fear.
Stage fright gets the best of me.
It's my time to belt out a song,
But my vocal cords rust over,
And whenever I try to speak,
The cords break,
And red wine spills out on my cream carpet.

Driving past homes,
Every motion-sensor light switches on.
All eyes are on me.
I wish I could hide from the recognition,
But the recognition saves me
When I'm tired of feeling like nobody notices me.

flu season

I'm so sick of
    fighting for you.

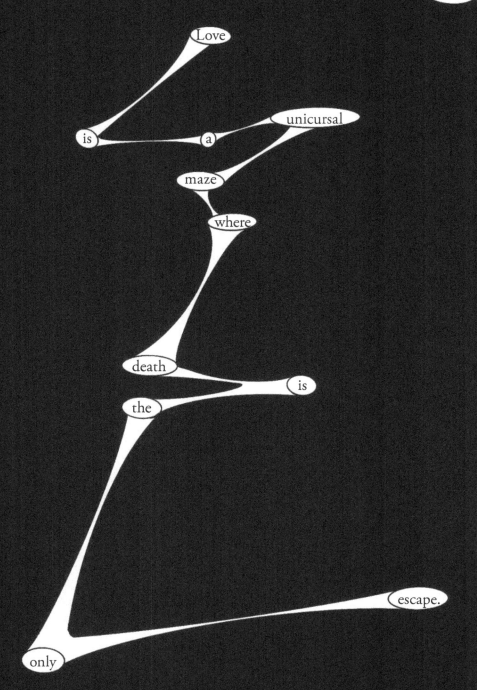

Love is a unicursal maze where death is the only escape.

masked

Friends aren't always what they appear;
Sometimes they're enemies disguised as your best friend.

mirror

Sometimes I talk to myself and act like I'm talking to you.

But if I was talking to you, I wouldn't be as open and honest

About how I was feeling.

Sometimes I talk about what I ate for lunch

Or the feelings I get when I fail my history tests.

Sometimes I get caught talking to you,

But I forget that means I'm talking to me too.

eighteen

'Cause now I'm eighteen,
Still talking like I'm fourteen,
Trying to live inside the daydream
Of the perfect first love story.
But when I wake up, it's a nightmare,
Talking myself off a ledge
Because I'm too scared
To go to school and face everyone who knew of us.

They all still talk about it
Like it was yesterday,
And I'm fond of the memories,
But I'm eighteen,
And I need to stop talking like I'm fourteen.

clown

I'm sorry that I'm not the friend you
wanted me to be.

I'm sorry that I was the friend that I
needed.

I'm sorry that I tried to be a good
person when it was hard to be.

I'm sorry that I'm such a bad person
because I did something good for you
and then criticized me for doing it.

You called me a joke because I did
what was right.

I guess the joke really is on me.

hope

Hope's for suckers

Who end up in gutters,

Who hate others

And don't have lovers.

the funeral

Have you ever thought about who's going to cry at your funeral?
Because I have.
It's an obsessive thought,
And honestly, I can't imagine anyone crying for me.
I feel like I'm just living to be an inconvenience,
Feeling like all my friends, who tell me that
      they love me, won't actually care,
That they'll just move along with their day.
That all my favorite teachers won't care either,
That I'm just a seat that fills up their classroom chair,
That I'm just another person's homework to grade,
That even when I get special treatment from them,
They won't actually care if one day I don't show up.
That my family would just sit and stare,
That I wouldn't be there at their dinner table,
That it wouldn't matter since I'm just another mouth to feed,
That my dog won't whimper or cry even though
      she knows something's wrong,
That when I don't come home, I'm just on vacation,
Only this time, for eternity.
Will anyone tell her that I found a home and live six feet under?

Have you ever thought about who's going to cry at your funeral?
Really think about who comes to your mind.
Is it your best friend?
Or her boyfriend that you're cool with?
Or the cheer team?
Or the coach?
Or the theatre kids and the director of the play you were cast in?
Or that leadership position you have?
Will they make a tribute?

Will they care?
Or will they all just say "Wow, that's awful.
   Anyways, the lesson today is…"
And continue with their day?

Have you ever thought about who's going to cry at your funeral?
Because I have.
I hate that I think about it
As often as I do.
I hate that I obsess about it.
I hate that I care about it.
I hate that even when I wouldn't care if anyone cried,
   I still wish someone would shed a tear.
I hate that I change who I am just to get a laugh out of someone.
So do I make a dramatic ending to get an audible
   gasp or weep from the audience?
Or do I just die silently, not wanting to disturb anyone's day?

People cry at movies or books when their favorite
   character has been killed off,
But what happens when you're nobody's favorite character?
When you're the villain of the century?
And the villain in your own eyes?
Do people cheer?
Since nobody cries for a villain.
So when someone asks if I think about it,
I say yes
And continue to obsess over the fact that
   nobody cried at my funeral.

decisions

"You will remember
The decisions you made
Right now
For the rest of
Your life."

I might if I don't die
Right now.

Because
If I'm dead,
Then
I won't remember the decision
To end it all.

fourteen

I thought that one day after we met,
You'd ask me to marry you years down the road,
So I stayed in the same place, waiting for you.
But what did I know
When I was fourteen,
Trying to live in a daydream?
The night came,
And the monsters came out to play,
And they all looked like you.

You always texted me the night before to wear my hair curly
So you could twirl your fingers through it during ninth period.
I thought it was so romantic;
I thought you never said it to anybody else.
But what did I know since I was only fourteen?
In high school where people tell me how to act,
Living in the same place at a new time,
Where there are new friends and relationships to force.

At every Friday-night football game,
You yelled at me, so I yelled back at you.
There was screaming and tears flowing,
Filling up the glasses we drank from on our date the next day.

We grew up, and I drove to see you at midnight every night.
Your friends are my friends,
And my friends call me a disaster
For being attached to someone who was never there.

free

I fill my brain with sound
So I can drown out your words.
It's hard to say this,
But I hate the person you became.
You aren't the same.
You fill my heart with negative doubt.
I try my hardest to make it far,
But I know I'll just end up in your car.

You made this scar.
I hate the person you became
Because you told me lies that were part of some game.
I took all the blame;
I carried all your shame.
I still want you now,
But I need to be free.

relapsed

I haven't gone back,
Not since the end of last year.
The scars are fading away.
I can't feel the scabs hanging off my heart.
I miss you.
I miss the roughness that your blade left.
I miss the crimson pooling out of my core,
        reaching the end of my body.
I miss the fact that no one knew,
But now everyone knows
'Cause I'm with you.

I haven't gone back since the end of last year.
It's something to be proud of, but every day
And every disappointment gives me a reason to run back to you.
"It's only this one. That's it."
Then that one turns into two,
Then three,
Then we fight and make up, and I'm left a bloody mess.

I haven't gone back since the end of last year.
And I feel like backsliding because my life
        tended to be good when I did.
The blood still stained my body as I walked into school.
I miss you,
But I won't relapse.
I can't do it
Because once I relapse,
There's no turning back.

ugly girl

I was never a good flyer;
I wasn't the best dancer.
I wasn't ever considered pretty
Or called beautiful.

Nobody ever wished they had the features I had
Or compared themselves to me,
And if they did,
It was only so they could feel better about themselves.

I wasn't considered ugly;
I was only the "conventionally attractive."
The type of "art piece" girl you think is beautiful from far away,
But when you walk up real close,
She's a mess,
And you need to wash your eyes out with bleach.

With all your stares,
Your eyes tell a story, sharing "The Tale of the Ugly Girl."
You call her by my name
And force her dialogue to say "I am an ugly girl
Because that's what everyone likes to call me."

You keep her in the cage you made,
Heckle her, and have people pay to make fun.
You push her against lockers,
Watch her slide down them in pain.
People gather around,
And suddenly you're the center of attention.
That's a lot of eyes on a girl whom you call ugly.

five o'clock

I'll be dead at five o'clock;
You have till then to say "so long."

I know that you'll be gone at five o'clock,
So I'll cry the night before dawn.

I'll cry before five
Because why would I cry when you're gone?

ex

Don't
you
forget
that
I
love
you
so
much,
but
now
that
I'm
doing
better,
you're
just
sad
I'm
not
in
your
arms.

smile

Heart pumping blood
Hurts my head,
Hurts my veins.
Breathe in and out,
Light-headed, hyperventilated.
Curled on the bathroom floor,
Not crying or screaming, staring.
"Why care when no one else does?"
Flip of a switch, and I'll be gone.
I wish it was that easy.
A snap of a finger, and I disappear
Out of existence.

Standing here, smiling,
Hurts my face,
Makes me feel worse,
Stretching muscles that I haven't used since last June.
Smiling faces gather around me.
"Why don't you just pull the corners of your
        mouth up. It's that easy."
Safety-pinned face now bleeds when my mouth goes neutral,
No more emotions,
Just blank.
Mushed-brain fool,
Brainwashed by the happiness of the people around me,
But when you really look,
They're all bleeding, too,
Sewed smiles permanently stuck to their flesh.
Forever happy even when depressed.
I guess everyone feels the same,
Concluding with the generations

That don't feel the need to discover the chaos that stalk their minds,
And when we ignore the disarray,
We find new ways
To stain smiles on faces
Even when their skin is splattered red.

manipulation

I cry when I'm sad;

I cry when I'm angry.

But I never got my way when I laughed, giggled, and
was generally glad.

So I cried when I wanted something,

Manipulation at its finest.

Shed many tears to drown out my sorrows even though
many of those tears weren't true.

I still showed them to you.

And after I stormed away upstairs,

I turned around.

A smile grew because I know that disappointing me was
something you didn't dare to do.

obsession

Arranging things on my
desk perfectly like so.

Everything is straight
and tidy like a bow.

OCD

- Growing up in a household where your issues are laughable
- Talking about OCD is just as funny as people dancing about the round table
- Compulsions that give me the nickname of freak
- But when I laugh at their pain, I'm psychotic and weak
- Checking behind my clothes in my closet to make sure someone isn't in my room
- Throwing back the shower curtain because I feel like I'm close to laying in my tomb
- And God forbid me getting caught doing these things
- Since everybody in this house is, apparently, perfect queens and kings
- I'm not saying this to be salty
- But this family is a bit faulty
- When it comes to the mental-health issues that are serious enough for me to want to cut my hands off because there are five fingers on one hand instead of four.
- Yeah, that was a mouthful
- And yes, I know you don't care
- But if you did
- Then you would be one step ahead of my mother and father dear
- Not all the obsessions are as "normal" as these
- And now this poem is going to have to freeze
- Since making a scene is not a pristine thing to see
- Now since we're talking about OCD
- You might not have noticed that there are twenty lines in this poem instead of nineteen.

the one

I lived my life making sure I died for all your lies.

I tried my hardest to let you know that you meant the world to me.

Whenever I did something to make you laugh,

You swung your fist back around just to watch me cry.

Kneel for the injured; don't let people make rumors.

Don't say anything to anyone; you'll survive the photographers.

I gave my existence to you,

And you walked away like I was nothing.

I gave my whole heart, mind, and soul to this,

And when it was all said and done,

You called me again

Just to make sure that I never forgot that you were the one.

god

I want to create an empire
Where everyone falls on their knees to worship me,
Singing prayers all pointed at me.
But I can never create one
Because I'm not that lucky.
If I was,
You would've never been in my life.

i'm stumped

I'm stumped.
I can't find the right words;
Everything that comes out just sounds like an alphabetical blur.
I want to say something meaningful,
But everyone judges you based on it.
And normally, I don't care,
But the judges and juries are also my executioners.
I want to write like it doesn't matter what I say
Since you'll find meaning when there isn't a meaning to say.
Everybody looks at me with a sideways glance,
Like I go around walking on walls.
You guys don't even give me a chance.
I said it once, and I'll say it again:
I'm stumped.
I'm tired of trying to figure out what to say when I've said it already.
Using different words and syllables doesn't change the fact
    that I walk around this earth constantly unsteady.
There are twenty-six letters in the English alphabet,
But none of them work with the words that I try to say.
Everyone walks around this world saying that
    I'm gonna get what I'm gonna get,
But they never look in the mirror and say the same.
I'm not calling everyone a hypocrite,
Yet that's hypocritical for me to say when that's exactly what I said.
Again,
I'm stumped.
The dots are on the page, but connecting them isn't the same,
Like that little game we all used to play,
A competition to see who's better at boxing people in.
It was just a game at first;
No one played it to get hurt.

You're probably wondering what I'm blabbering on about,
And honestly, I am too.
Because even after I wrote all these words
And rewrote them to make them rhyme,
They all mean nothing to me when I'm stumped out of mind.

nightmare

Why can't the day
just last forever?

At night, there are all
these horrors.

invisible people

I sit in silence

To fathom the loud, controlling
noise of my own head.

Something's going on.

I don't feel safe here;

I don't feel safe anywhere.

slice

S L I C E!
Cut the crease.
With every line I make,
The makeup bleeds.

S L I C E!
Make the lines straighter
Even if you cry
While smearing the concealer lines.

SLICE!
I hate this life.
Making my eyes longer,
Drawing on eyeliner
Makes me wanna die or cry harder.

sLICE!
One last cut of the crease.
Waterproof liner still lasts
If you cry while applying.

sliCE!
Even after the night is over
And the makeup comes off,
Piling up tissues,
The liner is still well-off.
Stained black lines
Last for eternity.

SLIce.
Life was good

When I put on the thick black lines.
Memories last forever,
Even when I cry on the bathroom floor,
Leaving the ink draining down.
Sketching on eyeliner
Makes me wanna drown.

Slice.
I hate applying eyeliner
Since I hated
Cutting the crease.

slice.

selfish

'Cause I'm selfish,

I can't believe you loved me for
    As long as you did.

Because I'm selfish.

Isn't that what you loved to say?

That I'm so selfish

For loving you the way you are.

school

I didn't add a class to my schedule for junior year;
I was told I might not get accepted into college.

I dropped a class from my schedule my senior year;
I was told I might not get accepted into college.

I'm failing my classes,
Everything but art and English.
I might not get accepted into college.
You tell me that and then say "Don't stress.
"There's always other options."

You fail me for something that wasn't assigned yet
Then don't answer my emails.
You tell me all these things and then tell me not to worry about it,
But I have an anxiety disorder
And OCD,
So I will stress over it
And then obsess over it,
Get new compulsions from the stress,
Obsess over the stress,
Stress over the obsession,
Obsess over the compulsions,
Stress over the obsession of the compulsions.

But wait, the people giving me the stress are also saying that I need
To calm down.
Thanks, everything is cured.

opinion

No matter what you think,
No matter what you say,
Your opinion of me
Means nothing to me
In any way.

i'll stop

I get made fun of for talking in complete sentences,
Called stupid, and told I was gonna fail.
Studying harder by the millisecond
Doesn't change the fate.

I get made fun of for using my calculator,
Like everyone has every problem figured out.
Two plus two doesn't always equal four when
    there are other signs attached to it.
So I punch in the numbers;
I have to make sure.

I get made fun of for writing notes in class.
Since I hear everything,
I should remember it,
Like the perfect student angels that I go to school with do.

I get made fun of for putting in 100 percent,
Being told to not try so hard,
To stop doing your homework and have a little fun.

I'll stop trying.
I'll stop writing notes.
I'll stop using my calculator.
I'll stop talking in complete sentences.

Great.
Failed.
You wanted?

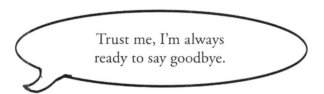

dead

What if he's dead?
What if the smile on my face shouldn't be there
But it's there because I don't know that he's gone?
Life is going too good;
The ear-to-ear grin should really shrink by this time of year.

What if he's dead?
What if he's six feet under and I didn't know?
What if that text you sent me two minutes before,
The one that said to call you,
Happened right before you died?
Because when I called you two minutes after,
There was no response.

What if he's dead?
What would I do?
Do I cry?
Do I show up at his funeral completely broken?
Or do I not show up at all?
And completely regret it for the rest of my life?

What if he's dead?
I haven't heard from him since that last text he sent me
About half an hour ago.

What if you're dead?
Do I start the memorial service even though
        I haven't seen the body?
Do I start making flower arrangements?
Or start writing the speech?

Who's going to get all your stuff?
What if I'm the only one who cares?
You weren't very liked.
What if I'm the only one who cries?

You're dead.
What do I do?
I haven't heard from you.
Do I scream silently because you never said goodbye?
Am I being interviewed by the police because I'm the last person
To hear from you?
Does anyone care?
Are you having fun up there?
Do you miss me?
Do you even know you're dead?

Oh,
Wait,
You responded.
You're alive.
Okay,
Back to the normally scheduled programming.

voice recording no. 2

I second guess everything
Only because I'm afraid of eating unhealthily.

romeo and juliet

A Romeo and Juliet romance,
More modern in the sense where we killed each other
Instead of ourselves,
Stabbed each other in the back,
And kicked in the shin.
We both came running back with a fake ear-to-ear grin.

A marathon that was endless
Until we became trapped in our homes,
Separated by the loveless disease;
There was no path back to you,
No matter how long I roamed.
I called out to you every day,
But the dove couldn't find its way.

Playing with our demons
Displayed out on the chess board.
King killed the queen;
Queen couldn't make her way to the horses.
Writing a murder in the Elizabethan era,
Adding symbolism in the text without knowing if it's correct.

Oh, Romeo, oh, Romeo, where art thou, Romeo?
Hiding behind the door?
Trying to give me a scare?
Oh, Romeo, you wouldn't dare!
I wouldn't play a trick on me
'Cause even you
I wouldn't spare.

A twisted love story always comes to an end
When one of them turns up dead.
Being dead doesn't mean six feet under;
I could mean change or sickness or something better.

But this love story I was trapped in
Was the beginning of my life.
However, I thought
The whole point of living was to not die.

Oh, Romeo, oh, Romeo,
I never heard from you again.
The locked doors clearly stopped you;
You knocked once and never did it again.

Oh, Romeo, oh, Romeo,
I hope your life is great.
I hope you found another Juliet
To torture, kill, and torment,
And I hope you remember that when you did it to me,
It made you very sick, oh, so frequent.

Oh, Romeo, oh, Romeo,
I can't wait to get revenge
Because our love story isn't finished until we both end up dead.

voice recording no. 3

I'd be locked in a mental institution
If I said half the things I thought of sharing.

observation

I've never drawn myself
Because I don't like staring at my complexion too long.
With every wrinkle and every freckle,
I just want to die
Because in my head,
Every part of me is terrible.

I wish I would be able to draw myself
Because sometimes I have a creative strike,
And I have the perfect reference picture for it.
But I will always search the internet
For hours on end
To find a similar reference
Just to prevent myself from death.

indomitable

It only took me thirteen seconds to fall in love with you
But thirteen years to forget the crevices in your hands.
And no matter how many pages I fill
Or how many pens run dry of ink,
I'll still fall in love with you
If you ask me to.

After all these years,
When time didn't fly
Since I didn't have fun,
I still remember your scar that runs deep
On the side of your left palm.

you

I can't distinguish what's right and what's you.

eggshells

Do you ever feel like you're walking on eggshells?
One crack, and everyone's head turns,
Staring daggers at you.
Can't slice the silence even with a butcher knife.
Shells sticking and splintering into your skin,
One more step, and everyone gets their pitchforks and fire ready.
Playing The Floor Is Lava
Is a better game to experience
Because you'd be burned by one step,
But the eggshells just burrow deep within
No matter how far you go.
One step, pain. Two steps, pain.
Walk a mile, same.
Can't share aspirations or dreams.
Can't spill secrets or anything mean.
I can just stand on the eggshells,
Get comfortable with the pain,
Because no matter what I say,
The blood will flow out every which way.
Praying won't get you anywhere,
Especially when you have a vendetta against God.
The Holy Trinity can't save you now,
Even when the eggshells are buried deep down.

love

I'd like to think of you as my first and forever love,
But you were more my salt-in-a-scratch love.
And as much as I want to keep you forever, love,
I have to cut the strings before I kill myself for love.

I would do anything for love.
Now I'm left burnt and cut.
But I did everything for you, my love.
Now I've gotta let it go before I lose it all
Because I used my heart instead of my head,
And I died because of what you called love.

text message no. 4

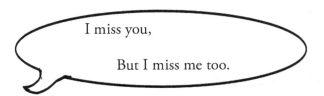

shield

I smile when I feel sad
Only so others don't have to ask.

When I feel depressed,
I hide my own emotions just to protect others.

the middle

I'd like to change
my inspiration.

I'd like to switch
the fact that I only
write about you.

I'd like to sing
about something
different.

But I can't because
you told me to
write

Before anyone else
did.

head and heart

The thing that pumps my blood
And keeps me alive
Is what kills me every time.
The thing that is protected by my rib cage
And could stop beating any second
Is the death of me every day.

The thing that's wrinkling
And pulses constantly in my head
Is what stops me from loving you.
The thing that makes the wheels turn
And makes me light-headed
Is what stops me from dropping everything
Just to be with you.

I follow one or the other.
I can't mix and match.
Think logically or with passion,
But don't think with both
Because when you do,
You end up drowning in never-ending seas
That stream from your eyes.

cheerleader

There were cheerleaders at my school who
told me,
"You would have potential if you didn't
look like you were on drugs half the time."
The worst part is
I'm a cheerleader.

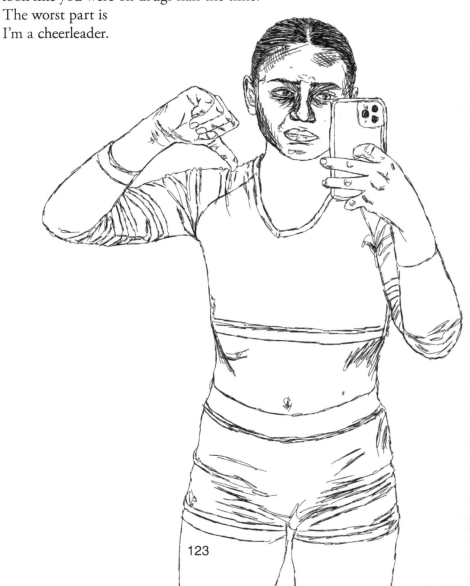

joker

Just a little joke,
A slight of breaking ice,
Getting laughter out of everyone in the room,
You turn my direction,
Lift up your arm,
And stretch out your finger.
Everyone behind you follows.
Loud exclaims of booming laughter
All directed at me.
Funny how the joke is always on me.
Funny how I'm always at the wrong end of the gun.
Funny how I'm still being blamed for you
putting me in this situation.
Funny how you still try to be in my life after you smashed it,
Put it back together,
And lit it on fire,
Just to watch me burn.

voice recording no. 4

'Cause people approach me,
Hate me,
But never love me.

imagination

Every day I see you walking by my home,
But all I wanted was for you to be my own.

I'd look at you out my window,
Daydreaming about our lives,
Until one day, you saw me and decided to stop by.

We started to talk, and my dreams became alive.
You were a brilliant little charm,
And I was safe in your arms.

We made people jealous,
But we didn't care
Because we were in love.

Soon enough, all my choices led only to a lie.
Now I'm dying inside.
You lied to me too many times.

I fell in love at fifteen, and now I'm broken at a half.
Every moment that we spent
Was all a lie, yet
I still want to believe that part of it was real.

Do what you want;

I'm the one who's gotta pay
attention to what's close to my wrists.

second place

You tell me I'm pretty,
But you call her beautiful.

You tell me I'm smart,
But she is always smarter in your eyes.

You tell me I'm skinny,
But she'll always be skinnier.

You tell me I'm everything
Until you see her.

I'm enough for you
Until you meet someone better.

I will always be second
In a life filled with number ones.

heartbroken girl

I see salt streams line down her face.
You ripped out her heart
And pulled it apart right in front of me.
I grabbed her hand,
Held it tight,
Walked her to the building
That didn't seem so far
In complete silence.
The three of us walked,
Running my thumb up and down
The length of the back of your hand,
Knuckles to wrist.
I hear you sniffle back the tears.
Steps in sync,
We never looked anywhere else,
Just straight ahead.
Oh, heartbroken girl,
He didn't mean to make you cry,
But he can't open his heart up
And express the love no matter how many times he tries.
Oh, heartbroken girl,
Your first love shouldn't have ended like this,
but it did.
And one day it won't feel as wrenching
As it does right now.
It'll get easier.
You watched me feel the same way,
Only many times more,
But I feel okay now,
Even if my heart is still torn.

love story

Can't decide if you love me or want me dead.
This love is bipolar; I can tell you from experience.
Happy one second,
Turn around, and we're throwing tables
And screaming at the top of our lungs,
Crying and breaking the pictures that we hung,
Taking a break and coming back home after months.
Yeah, this is love.

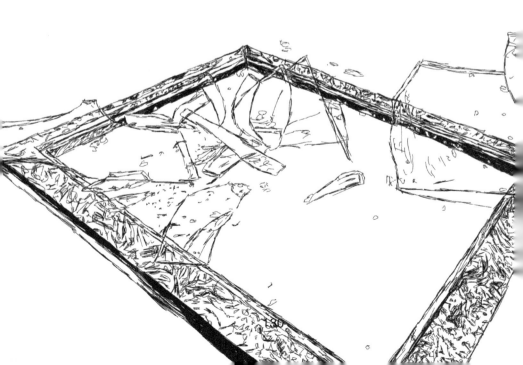

JL part 2

I hope you still love me as much as I love you.

I hope you forgive me just like I always do.

I hope you still miss me as much as I do.

I hope you still love me even though you never do.

I never want to hate me, yet I always do.

I never want to hurt you, but somehow, I always do.

I want you to miss me as much as I miss you.

marathon

You said this was temporary,
But I've been like this for four or five years,
And it seems like there's no end in sight.
So it might be better if I just died.
There's always a light on the other side of the tunnel;
I might as well run there instead of taking my time.

enemy

Alone.
Dark rooms.
Long hallway.
Balcony.
Dark figure.
Blood.
Pain.
Death.
The devil came for me;
He wanted me dead.
He killed me because I was more evil than him.
Instead of an alliance,
He became an enemy.
Alone.
Dark rooms.
Long hallway.
Balcony.
Dark figure.
Blood.
Pain.
Death.
All because he was my enemy.

slapstick tragedy

Horror movies aren't comedy productions
When you're living inside of one.

invasion

Words are my safe space,

Yet you use them as a weapon.

So sadistic, I can't take it.

ailment

You're the monster living in my head.
Insomnia controls me;
I lie awake waiting
For someone to save me
From my sleeplessness.
When the middle of the night becomes the middle of the day,
Constant blame,
As if I asked for all of it,
But I'll fall asleep some time.
It'll be okay.

numb

Feeling nothing is a blessing in disguise.
Imagine feeling every pin of pain stabbed in your arm.
Imagine feeling someone rip out your heart,
Sew it back in,
And tear it out once more.
Imagine having someone take away every person you cared about
Purely because they hate you so much,
Even after all you did was love them.
I felt every single shred of pain you caused me,
But once the tears dried
And the pain washed over,
I felt nothing but the deep black hole where my heart,
That you used to love
Used to be.
And after all this time
And every tear spilled,
All I get to say is "I'm fine."

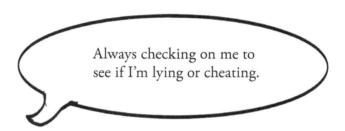

attached to imprisonment

I guess loving you was a crime,
So lock me up
And throw away the key.
"I don't need a man,"
Says stupid old me.
But when I get lonely
And don't know what to do,
I go running back to you.

fatigued phobophobia

Eyes are always blurry;
I can't see straight.
I'm tired of the tears falling,
And I'm tired of being afraid.

anticipation

Waiting for your call is like waiting for my death date.

Expecting something from you is like waiting for
    eternity, just to be killed by my fate

Because you didn't mean anything you said.

You built up my love and then left me to fend for myself,

And I don't know how you could feel so great

When you left me with my heart breaking,

Shattering on the ground,

Running through broken glass and sand

Just to find out that you're nowhere around.

everything you told me

A: "And why would I care?"
B: "Because you mean a lot to me."
C: "Caring about you is how I spend my day."
D: "Do you think I would lie to you?"
E: "Everyone here stares at us."
F: "F——ck you."
G: "Good night, baby girl. I'll see you tomorrow."
H: "Hey, I miss you."
I: "I love you, baby."
J: "Just believe me!"
K: "Killing me."
L: "Love me like I love you."
M: "Many friends from many different places."
N: "No, we're done."
O: "Out of everyone here, you're my favorite."
P: "People don't get an opinion of you."
Q: "Question after question, just stop!"
R: "Right, and I'm lying to you?"
S: "Stop lying!"
T: "Then leave!"
U: "Understand that I would never lie to you."
V: "Very funny."
W: "Wear your hair curly tomorrow."
X: (Your vocabulary isn't big enough for a word starting with *X*.)
Y: "You're being dramatic."
Z: "Zero reasons why you should feel like that."

joke

It's funny when you
walk through your
life believing that
everyone hates you.

It's even funnier when
it's true.

return

Please stay connected.
Keep calm and collected,
Like I always do.

Read the terms and conditions.
If you don't, life's pessimistic.
I can't always lose.

I can feel my heart
Beating out of my chest.
I won't cut my losses.
Yet I always do.

As much as I complain about you,
I always find a way to run back to you.

romance tales

All the "I'm sorrys" and promises you made
During the late-night phone calls
Where you were stuck in a daze.

I wish you remembered what you said.
I wish it was as vivid in your head
As it is in mine.

Screaming and blaming me for all your wrongs,
Acting as if I begged for this all.

Trapping me in corners,
Saying that you forgive it all,
Every lie that you said and every time that I called.

Our eyes couldn't break;
The mold was already made.

Sliding down the wall that you pushed me against.
Teardrops running away from me.

All I say is I'm sorry
And hope you forgive me for the actions you made.

paranoia

Look out the window; make sure nobody's there.
Get out of bed; walk to the bathroom.
Check behind the shower curtain; make sure nobody's there.
Get ready for the day.
Look out the window before I walk out the front door;
Make sure nobody's there.
Get in my car, check the trunk, check the back seat,
Make sure nobody's there.
Look under the car, look under the seat,
Make sure there's nothing there.
Drive to school, look in the mirror,
Make sure there's nobody following me.
Get to school, get out of the car,
Lock it once, lock it twice,
Make sure nothing can get in.
Go to class, sit in the back,
Make sure nobody stares at me.
After school, go to my car; the same schedule follows.
Drive home from school, a different way every day,
Make sure nobody can say that I stick to a schedule.
Get to my neighborhood, drive the block,
Make sure nothing is out of place.
Get to my house, park my car, lock it, same way as I did before.
Go inside, get the knife, and check behind every door.
Do my homework, check the doors,
Take a shower, check the curtain.
Go to bed, check the closet, turn out the lights.
Get up the next day, do it all again.
It's tiring, yes,
But I do this all because of my paranoia.

mercy

Big chance,
I can't wait for this romance.
I can't wait to go see you,
Knowing that I don't need you
'Cause you know you've got a bad vibe,
Knowing I mess with the bad guys.
You hope that you don't see me
'Cause you'll end up on your knees,
Begging me for mercy.

indecisive

I'm inside my own mind;
I don't know what to do.
I don't understand what's wrong and what's right.
I can't decide to be evil or to be nice.
I could commit murder, and no one would know
Because the secrets I carry are buried
Deep down inside my soul.
I don't know what to do
When there are so many voices only yelling out for you.
I don't know what do to when it's only I who stands alone.

too bad

Mother, father—arguing in the kitchen,
And they wonder why I lack empathy.

Looking at me, they see
A bloodstained face
And me in my casket, wearing black lace.

Too bad your friends picked me in the divorce.
Too bad that you found out from an outside source.
It's too bad that my heart breaking threw your life off course.

It's too bad, but it's hard for me to care
'Cause you left me teary and stumbling home to my lonesome.
Too bad your friends cared that I was lonely.

Rude awakening,
'Cause now I get nervous that it's your number
That's calling me at one a.m., telling me to come over.

'Cause, baby, I get nervous that it's you coming to get me.
I bite my nails until they bleed.
Too bad it was your friends who were there to comfort me.

Eight hundred people in one room

And somehow, I ended up with you

possibilities

Yes, I know it's not true
Since I'm lying to you
And I'm lying to me too.

But if it was the whole truth,
What would you do?

toxicity

You are toxicity at its finest.
You are the worst possible thing for me to indulge on,
Yet
I do it anyways.
An addiction.
A drug.
You are toxicity to me.
I am allergic to the way you live.
I get hives at the way you speak.
My throat closes up when I see you walking towards me.
You are toxicity in my eyes.
You are the blade that slices through my skin.
You are the addiction I indulge in so I don't hurt as much.
You are the Band-Aid that I rip off my skinned knee.
You are the duct tape that tears off my mouth.
You are a drug that I can't go to rehab for
Because nobody knows you exist.
You are toxicity at its finest.

examination

I make plans with everyone,
But then I get this overwhelming feeling of
"I don't wanna go."
Am I afraid of leaving my house?
Am I afraid of people?

I don't know.

death date

Packed my bags, I'll be gone by tomorrow.
See, this date only brought me sorrow.
Feelings so deep, it's like they're gone.
I guess all the emotions shared are done.

déjà vu

All you men, all the same,
None of you have ever changed.
    Once I get away from you,
    I turn around,
    Damn,
    Déjà vu.

mind changer

You want to be my friend;
I like you just fine.
You ask me to dance;
I say "Sure, go ahead."
You ask me out on a date;
I respectfully decline.
Now you're acting like you never said anything,
Ignoring me because you know you did.
You're acting different,
So I did too.
Now you're mad at me because I started ignoring you.
"Do you want to hang out?"
"I don't think that's a good idea."
"Why am I even surprised?"
No answer.
Wants to save me but also hates me.
Wants to love me but can't even act right around me.
Wants to be the best person in the world for me but acts like
The person I despise the most.
Wants everything from me but doesn't give me anything in return.
Remember when I said nobody cares
And you tried to convince me that you do?
Remember when I said that everyone says they do until they don't
And you tried to tell me that you'll care forever because
I don't understand how much you care about me in the first place?
Do you remember that?
Because I do.
Now I sit alone,
Thoughts running marathons in my head,
And I only think of those conversations you don't remember
And think I am crazy instead.

Because when you said you'd care forever,
Forever never ended,
But your promise sure did.
So here I am,
Standing alone,
With the mentality that nobody cares.
And after this experience,
Like the many others before,
I remember why this mentality stays present in my mind
For eternity.

He's sitting with his girlfriend, and he texts
Me, "I love and miss you, baby girl."

angel view

Sometimes I wish you were here
with me.

Sometimes I wish you were alive
to see

All the awful things he did to me,

All the horrible things, every
awful speech,

Although I'm sure you can see
every piece breaking off me.

I'm sure you can see me in pain
when the ends don't meet.

too young

I told my mom I don't believe in love;
She said I'm too young for that.
But I'm old enough to understand
That love and hurt go hand in hand.

line

You wanted my heart;

That was where I drew the line.

You didn't like that I drew it

So close to all the principles

I used to let you define.

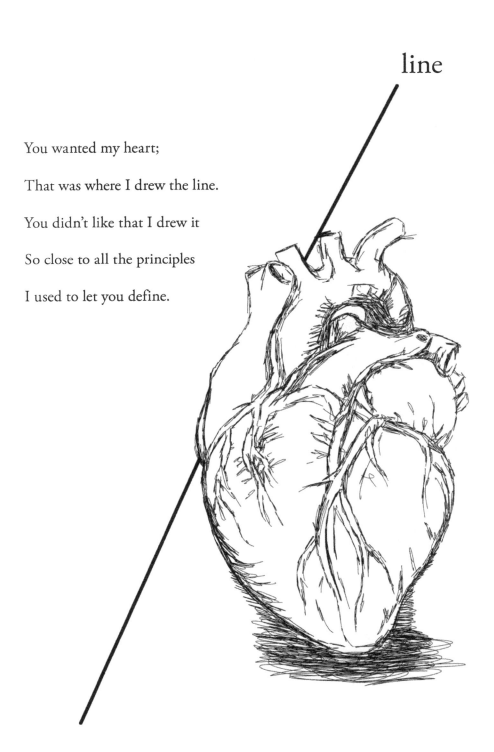

dying inside

Please stop asking me if I'm mad or if I'm fine
When it's perfectly clear I'm dying inside.

sonnet

Pass the ball, throw her higher, be better.
Or don't try at all, be nice, not too nice,
These rules, stereotypes, stuck in fetter;
No matter what I do, I don't suffice.

Reprimanded like I'm a young child,
Expected to be an adult, full grown.
Treated poorly, everything but mild.
Be this or be that, "When I'm here, dethrone."

Whispers go around; hatred fills the air.
"Evil beyond my mind"; lies set my theme.
All coming towards me, life isn't fair.
Trapped in my sinful head, no split in seams.

And, yet, mirrors are present, and I see
A girl crying from perceptions of me.

pretend

I'm saying "I guess" because you treat me atrociously.
You ignore me, and I know you're on your phone because
    you're always on it when you're with me.
We used to talk every day, but now we don't talk at all.
I'm lucky if I hear from you at all.
I no longer mean anything to you,
When you used to say I was the only person you talk to anymore.
You used to say our friendship would never
    end, and now we never speak.

I've said this before, but you're not listening.
I'm tired of being drained by not knowing if you'll respond or not.
I care about you more than you ever cared about me.
I've accepted that already, but it still hurts.
I couldn't sleep, I couldn't cry, I just felt empty.
I was feeling so low, and I can't even talk to you anymore.
I'm just by myself because everybody else has left me already too.

I still smile to pretend I'm fine, but I lost my best friend,
Who doesn't care about me anymore.
I want to say I won't ever leave you,
Even though you're always leaving me,
But that's not fair to me.
So I'm learning to live without you.

text message no. 9

God, she is like me,

Her eyes, her beauty, her ability to love you
after everything you did.

dreamers

LA, Paris, and New York,

Places we talked about visiting together.

It's funny how we planned our whole
lives together when we were only fifteen.

angel

Because while the tears come soaring down her face,
I'm the one to clean up the mess because you can't embrace.
With all your yelling and screaming,
She can't take it anymore, so one day,
She goes to explore how to fly.
Her wings took her so high.
Now she can't remember why she didn't do this before.

I don't want to blame you,
But it's your fault that she hates you
As much as she does.
'Cause birds can only soar as high as the space that you give them,
But angels can fly higher than the sky,
And you pushed her so you could see
How much space was given to breathe.

With all your yelling and screaming,
She can't take it anymore, so one day, she goes to explore how to fly.
Her wings took her so high.
Now she can't remember why she didn't do this before.

Calling her overdramatic as if she didn't hear
But you said it as loudly as someone who doesn't care.
Now she's flying higher than she ever did before.
I don't want to blame you, but she did this since you were here.

lucid

I love that feeling when I wake
Up and it's just a dream.

And you didn't actually come
and find me.

That you didn't figure out my
number

Or the school that I'm going to.

circles

Because I'm tired of wasting paper, writing about you.
I'm tired of talking about my past
Like I didn't mean anything to you.
But I still count the days down
Till I get your message,
Wishing me a happy birthday.
Then the whole thing starts again.

voice recording no. 5

'Cause I changed the way I looked just for the validation,
I changed my whole life for the accommodation,
And I still wasn't enough to be with you.

heartbeat

I'm fond of practicality.
I'm protective of my boundaries,
Yet I lose all my sense when it's
You and me
And it's your hand
In mine.
I get confused
When my heart is on the line.

Obviously, I fall in love with the
wrong people

Because obviously, I fell in love
with him.

lonely

Every tear that I shed,

Every night that I spent

Sitting alone in my room,

Waiting for you to assume

That I lied when I talked to you.

lying to myself

I don't cry over things that I never had,

But every night,

Salt streams down my face

Because I thought I had you

When I never did.

And I'd rather die

Than admit I was wrong,

And I'd rather lie

Than admit I wasn't strong.

deserved collapse

One thing could go wrong,
And
Poof,
Your whole world collapsed.

But never talk about the struggle;
Don't talk about emotions.
Keep your head up,
And never let your eyes show your pain.

Don't share your depression;
Everything bad that happens
Happens to you for a reason.

You deserve it,
And don't say you don't deserve it
Because you do.

Even if you're the best person to ever exist,
You deserve everything bad that happens
Purely based on the fact that your friends are
      imitations of the real thing,

And they'll do anything to you if you let them.
Even if you say they're terrible for doing the actions,
They'll always convince themselves they did it for you,
Even when they only did it for them.

calligraphy

I wish we went back to old times,
When handwritten love letters were the way you told me
You loved me.
But now I only get messages on text.
The little three dots can't help me now
When my mind makes conspiracies
And I want to end my life by drowning
Out every word
And every lie
You said to me.

never again

When I said "Never again,"
I wish I meant it every time I said it.

When I said "Never again,"
I meant that I never wanted to fall down
The never-ending rabbit hole of pain and misery
Just to end back inside your arms.

voice recording no. 6

I didn't like the way my face looked when I was smiling,

So I stopped.

perjury

'Cause I used to hear my phone ring in the dark.
I used to rush to your house anytime you needed my heart,

And I used to tell you how much I loved your "art,"
But it's interesting how my feelings can change overnight.

Ignoring the truth until the truth was hard to hide.
We used to talk every day, and now nothing's the same
Because you lied about yourself,
And I lied to save the same.

blame

I really like how you blame my intuition
    for something that you did.

I wanted to live in the moment, but the
    moment's coming to an end.

I really like how you blame this situation as something that I did.

I wanted to live forever with you, but forever's come to an end.

i remember when i was nine

Sky filled with gray clouds,

Everybody's feeling down.

Do you remember what you said to me yesterday in the hallway?

You said, "I love you. Nobody can compare."

I guess that wasn't true

Since now you're with her.

I didn't want to admit that you were right;

I would've heard about it for the rest of my life.

I didn't want to say you're too good for goodbyes;

I would've regretted it for the rest of my life.

I thought our love was a movie,

Like the one we saw on our first date.

I thought our love was worth fighting,

But survival is a game,

So this is what I get for trying.

So what?

Did you just become the villain overnight or something?

I didn't become a villain overnight.
I needed to save myself from these people.

And the only way I could do that was
to become something that would make
them leave me alone.

the purge

If I could commit any crime,

Illegal or not,

I'd commit murder.

I'd stab you in the back,

Only once,

Just like you did to me,

Only a thousand times more.

tears

I've been going through the motions of the day.

I've been numb my entire life.

I wanna feel okay; I wanna feel alright.

Maybe leaving this world would clear my mind.

You broke me down,

Didn't help me up.

I cried to sleep;

My pillow soaked it up.

I wanted you with me,

But we're not soulmates in the slightest.

unchanged

The dark isn't any different when you close your eyes.

The night isn't any less terrifying if you hide under the covers.

Your love isn't any different if we never met in the first place.

The heartbreak isn't any less painful if I left after the first fight.

voice recording no. 7

Nostalgia is falling for people who remind me of you,

Loving people who didn't love me too.

six p.m.

I waited until the end of your practice.

Mom was yelling at me,

But I wanted to see you

Because you were a familiar face after a long, hard day of misery.

child

Mother and father always arguing down in the kitchen.
Everyone listens, but no one understands the condition.
This whole situation is a bit eerie;
I'm sitting here, acting like I'm watching a
      whole reality TV drama series.
I try to help, but you yell at me, saying that I'm just a child.
I just walk away, holding on to my fake smile.
Am I insane for having no reaction?
Am I broken because my heart is collapsing?
This pain soaks in my system daily;
I notice the anger rising as high as the Black Sea.
I've just been going through the motions as if my
      body's in the room, but I'm not really there.
I walk through the halls, numb as I can be
Because sometimes to stay alive, your mind has to flee.
I hope my parental figures know that my heart is not waterproof,
And so, *poof,*
There I go, leaving the past in the house by the
      Bay Bridge only a bit to the south.
Again, I try to help out or intervene.
Oh, but that's okay; go ahead and make a scene.
I guess I'll just wait to understand and grow,
But then again, what do I know?
When I'm just a child "pretending."

answers

Because I think I can solve all my issues by
Moving across the country.

Finding one love and staying with him forever.
Nobody ever turning our heads and us dancing down the aisle.

Because I think I can solve all my issues by
Being by myself.

Painting every wall black and ignoring every call.
Nobody comes to check up on me, and I
     find love by being by myself.

home to you

I remember the day we met,
First day of freshman year.
You asked me some dumb question,
But now I can't really remember.
I used to find you so exciting; you made me laugh.
Now I'm not sure.
My mind is forgetting details that I need
To get to you.

I smile at my nightmares;
Who cares if I drown?
When I wake up at three a.m.
And there's no one around,
I used to call you, so excited
About the drama that I heard,
And we'd endlessly gossip, but now all the lines are blurred.
I want to call you sometimes, but I can't find
        my way back home to you.

After three months of dating—wait, we never got that far.
I remember us dancing—no, wait, I think those were stars.
I'm sure I had fun,
But I can't remember the important things that got us this far.

I used to call you, and you'd answer,
And we'd gush about each other.
Now I look back at the past and see a bloodstained blur.
Yes, I still wanna call you sometimes,
But I got lost going home to you.

I remember the day we met.
We laughed during class and got yelled at by the teacher.
But I would take it all back if that means we didn't miss each other.
I wish I saw you coming back,
But I think there's no path going home to you.

I'm tired of everyone falling in love on the TV.

I'm tired of this not ever happening to me.

my life

I made you out to be my soulmate.
Soon enough,
I was stuck on the wrong side of the gate.

I wanted you to be
Next to me all my life,
But you're the wrong one for me.
It's my time to be free.
So let me leave to live my life.

I made you out to be my paradise,
And I'm paying the price
Because you made me cry.

All my tears are dry.
I'm falling for you,
So set me free
And let me leave to live my life.

the third friend

Middle-school days,
Awkward as always.
Duct-taped Converse shoes
So the rain doesn't come through.

Three girls walking in a line horizontally,
Only one girl walking on the grass cautiously,
Leaping over mud piles and rain puddles.
If I ask them to move over on the sidewalk,
It would only bring me troubles.
Walking behind them is the only way to be on cement
Because if I walk in front of them,
It will bring me emotional torment.
Either on grass or plaster,
My day will end up a disaster.

My friends in middle school were mean girls
Who made fun of me if my hair wasn't nice-looking in my curls.
I tried to contain the spectacle;
Once graduation hit, it was only ethical
To stop texting them and leave them grasping for my attention.
Move on to high school, to start all forms of new tension.

gone

Saying that I'm a complete person
Doesn't mean anything to me
When I feel so broken inside.

That piece of my heart that you broke
And took with you
After the first fight
Always comes back each time.

JL part 3

I fell in love with words that I'd heard before,

But you switched them around

Just so I could feel like I meant something more.

You told me not to worry,

Yet here I am,

Standing here, acting like I'm glad.

A sewed-on smile only works when I can't.

ghost

I know she knows I'm here.
She looks at me when I stand in front of her.
She feels my presence beside her
When I'm petting her hair
As the tears fall down her cheek.
She knows I'm holding her head lightly
When it hurts her so much
That she can hardly breathe.
She realizes that I read the books when she does the same.
She even pauses on the same page
Until I finish reading the frame.
Sometimes I get angry
And stare at her from the corner.
She turns around because she feels the tension.
She walks over to me and tries to comfort my being.
Sometimes I watch her wash her face and brush her teeth
Early in the morning.
Sometimes I see her pull out of the driveway and into the traffic.
I see her drive back home and go upstairs.
She slams her backpack on the ground,
Curls up into a ball on the floor.
Sometimes she hyperventilates.
Sometimes she just sits and stares;
I watch her all day.
I watch her all hours of the night.
No, I'm not her stalker.
I'm a ghost that lives to be her knight.

vending machine

The broken-down vending machine at my school doesn't
    pay cash, coins, credit card, or Apple Pay.
There isn't a sign that says Out of Order.
Every student and faculty member
Automatically knows that it's nonfunctional
When you walk by it on the way to class.
Sometimes you see someone new trying to make it work,
Jamming coins or shoving crumpled dollar bills in the slot,
But the machine doesn't take them.
It spits the money back out, and you're left
    trying over and over and over again
Until you see frustration growing on the kid.
They put the money back in their pocket,
Kick the machine,
Say a curse word, and roll their eyes.

Standing in the corner doesn't make you invisible.
Everyone knows you're there.
Everyone just ignores that fact.
I walk through the hallway where
The faulty vending machine stands.
I stare, wondering if it could feel my hand
Putting up the paper that everyone else can brush aside.
It's painful to watch something be shattered
And still be forced to stand at the ledge,
So I save the vending machine
By putting up the Out of Order sign.

text message no. 13

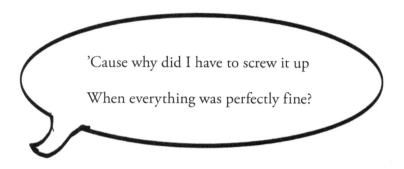

'Cause why did I have to screw it up

When everything was perfectly fine?

two people

Two people,
Never friends,
Poking fun
Even when one's down.

Two people,
Best friends
Hanging out
Even when depressed.

Two people,
Just strangers
Ignoring them
Even when sitting next to each other.

Two people,
Only acquaintances
Slowly talking
Even when there's no trust.

Two people,
Best friends again,
Always together
Even when our souls could never be farther.

time travel

If I could go back in time,
I'd do it all over.
I'd never fall for your smile
Or all the things you said because you knew what I wanted to hear.

If I could go back in time,
I never would've listened to you
When you sent me a heart or said "I love you"
Because now I know it was never true,
Because if you truly loved me like you said you did,
You never would have left your knife in my back,
And you never would've taken all my friends
Because they decided they liked you more than me.

If I could go back in time,
I would change every second
Because I would've rather been alone
Than with you again,
Because when you said that you'd love me forever,
I listened to it.

But if I could go back in time,
I would never listen to you again.

stay

Because I believe in
protecting my peace

After you left me dying
in pieces.

No, I didn't say to leave,

But when you hurt me,

It was hard to say

"Please stay.

"I don't wanna live my
days without you.

"Please stay.

"Without you, it gives me
no point in sticking
around.

"Please stay.

"I'd hate to live my life
with no one around to see
me.

"Please stay."

JL part 4

If you love me, let me know
Because I can't wait around forever,
Trying to convince myself that you love me
When you never did.

If you want me, let me know
Because I can lie to myself forever,
Trying to manipulate and gaslight every thought
that sweeps through my mind.

responsibility

Self-inflicted wounds,
Blaming myself for everything
That I do to myself,
As if you didn't help me resume.

Hurting me is like a game to you,
Acting like this is something you have to do.
Screaming and crying in A flat.
No matter how much we argue, you always come back.

voice recording no. 8

Bleach can get everything out,

But when I drink it,

I can't get you out of my mind.

you and me

I wonder how many times a night you think of me
Because I never stopped thinking of you.

I wonder how many times we looked at the same stars
Because I wished on all of them for you.

I need to see you every day;
I live and breathe just to see your face.

I know you don't feel the same
As I do.

I think long and hard and dream of you,
Acting like we're living somewhere where nothing compares
To the sight of you.

eating disorder

I felt guilty for eating
Because you guilt-tripped me into thinking
That I was the problem.

court

I'm not as important to you as previously stated.

"I love you" statements were in the terms and conditions.

I guess I need a lawyer to get you to keep your promises.

I'm tired of dealing with all my losses.

haunted mansion

When I was little,
I was terrified of the Haunted Mansion.
I was scared that I would never survive
Or that some demon was going to possess me
Or bury me alive.
But now that I'm older,
I realize none of that would be true.
And now that I'm older,
I really wish some of it would be.
I ride Haunted Mansion in hopes that I would die
Or never come out the same.
I remember crying,
Walking to the ride.
Once I got off,
The tears dried,
And I felt nothing like the same.
All my hoping paid off
Because I came out differently.
Then when I strolled in
When I was little,
I was terrified of the Haunted Mansion.
Now that I'm a teenager,
The Haunted Mansion is my favorite ride.

voice recording no. 9

I wish I could go back to ninth-grade year
So I could switch it all around,
Just so you never appeared.

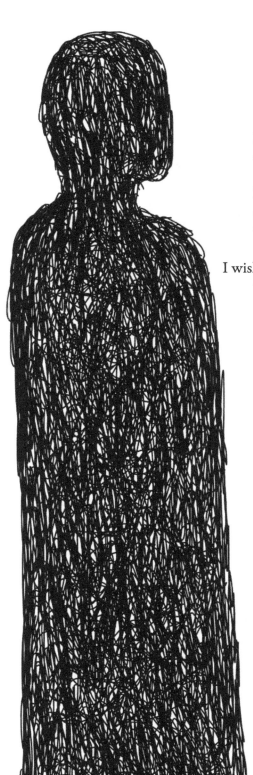

no identity

Every time I saw you, I
changed the way I acted.

Now I act like you're
always gonna be there even
when I know you never are.

I wish I never changed, and I
wish I stayed
unapologetically me.

countdown

I almost died at birth.

It's a shame that it didn't
happen, because I count the
days down until I'm gone.

dramatic

"Everyone needs to stay off the roads.
"There will be high wind,
"Constant rain,
"And massive amounts of flooding."
No matter which news station I click through,
They're all talking about the storm,
Cancelled sports events, and locked down at home.
"The storm will start at two."
Counting down the hours of the day
To stay inside,
Peeking out the dusty white blinds
To witness the level 5 storm on the impact scale,
Something that California has never seen before.
Similar to the pandemic,
Possibly more dramatic
Since we shut down school
Far faster than COVID ever did.
A theatrical performance from every
News anchor and meteorologist,
I'd give it five stars and an Oscar if I could
Since the storm never showed
When everyone said it would.

multiples

I just want to leave,
Leave this school,
Leave this house,
Leave this city, this state even.
Leaving, everyone is so good at leaving.
I tend to be left,
Left heartbroken.

I just wish someone,
Somewhere,
Would stay with me.
My friends say all the stuff that happens to me is just my luck.
I make bad decisions,
And I deserve all the pain that comes my way.

Switching from manic to depressive
In a split second,
Having two separate worldviews.
One life,
One personality,
Two worldviews,
Confused and lonely in both.

voice recording no. 10

Working on yourself never works out
    When you weren't the problem
    To begin with.

ZR part 2

Met you a few weeks ago,
Fell so hard, I didn't even know what hit me.
Laughed and cried and danced all night,
I was yours, and you were mine.
I didn't even notice that she was the noise
    sneaking around the back.

I just wanna be free;
I just wanna be me.
I don't wanna miss my chance to escape while
    I'm begging on my knees.
No, you didn't have to cheat.
You could've just told me,
But you chose to be a liar.

I asked if you were seeing her,
Blamed and tortured by your words.
"Friends don't lie." Yeah, that's for sure.
Thought you were mine and I was yours.
Buckets dripping with my tears.
You walked away and went with her.

No, you didn't have to cheat.
You could've just told me,
But instead, you chose to mess me up inside my head.
You cheated, and I apologized instead.

text message no. 14

I can't even look you in your eyes and tell you that I'm scared,

'Cause you'd laugh it off and tell me you never cared.

deservance

"Let's hang out!
"I haven't seen you in forever."
It's funny how those words haunt me,
As I see you blocked me
From your life, story being shared to everyone but me.

In a split-second shot,
You decided to be
A foe rather than a friend.

It doesn't matter that I have pictures
From every day we spent
Together, making fun of him and the way his hair went.

Now I'm by myself,
Ready to send
A whirlwind of calmness
Since karma told me to back down as she extends
Her hand of deservance over the boyfriend and girlfriend.

Horns sound and alarms go off,
All because they're crying
From the torture of karma,
And I'm still well-off.

permanence

Arguments turn to screaming matches.

I live my life with permanent heart scratches.

don't worry

I was slut-shamed and hated on for
loving you,
As if loving you was a choice that I chose
to do.

But don't you worry;
Your reputation is fine.
It's not like you live your days with
teary eyes,
Remembering our goodbyes.

disguise

Because after you broke my heart,

You asked me if I was okay,

And

I said "I'm fine"

With tears running down my face.

Snide remarks at me

But of course, if I say anything to her about it,

I'm being dramatic, and I'm gaslighting her, or I'm lying.

death of my past

This doesn't change anything,
You looking at me.
Your smile still makes me laugh,
But I guess that's because I'm still in love with you.

And I hate to admit it because you killed who I was.
Yes, I remember when me met,
And I remember every time you left,
And I hate that I love you
After leaving you responsible for the death of my past.

told

I've been told
My entire life
To believe in myself
And ignore everyone else's insight.

I've been told
My entire life
To not love easy
And not trust anyone who loves you hard.
But then
Here you are,
Strolling in my life
Like you owned it before you even knew me.

the ending

Now I write poems about you for a living.

I wanted more material, but you said I was digging.

I wish I didn't feel like I owed you something for your time.

Because even after all the tears and all the goodbyes,

I feel like you were the mastermind

Because you told me to write.

about the author

Katherine Cava was born and raised in the San Francisco Bay Area, California. She attended Moreau Catholic High School and currently attends Penn State. She's studying criminology, prelaw, and creative writing. She is the well-known "art kid" around school and spends most of her time working on portfolios and making posters to post around school. She also finds constant comfort in the safety of her notes app, where she finds the strength to embrace the hard-to-come-by emotions. She writes and draws about a number of topics, including heartbreak, mental health, movie scenes, songs, and many others.

9 798889 604792